Colonial People

The *Milliner*

Niki Walker & Bobbie Kalman

Illustrations by Barbara Bedell

 Crabtree Publishing

www.crabtreebooks.com

Created by Bobbie Kalman

Dedicated by Niki Walker

To Nicole McGuire, a woman of great style

Editor-in-Chief
Bobbie Kalman

Writing team
Niki Walker
Bobbie Kalman

Copy editors
Kathryn Smithyman
Amanda Bishop

Computer design
Margaret Amy Reiach
Robert MacGregor (cover)

Production coordinator
Heather Fitzpatrick

Photo researchers
Heather Fitzpatrick
Jaimie Nathan

Consultant
Jan Shipway

Printer
Worzalla Publishing
Company

Digital prepress
Embassy Graphics

Photographs and Reproductions
Colonial Williamsburg Foundation: title page, pages 4, 8, 13, 14, 15 (both), 16, 20, 26, 31
Charles Willson Peale, *Portrait of John and Elizabeth Lloyd Cadwalader and Their Daughter Anne* (detail), Philadelphia Museum of Art: Purchased for the Cadwalader Collection with funds contributed by the Mabel Pew Myrin Trust and the gift of an anonymous donor: page 5
Smithsonian American Art Museum, Washington DC / Art Resource, NY: John Singleton Copley, *Mrs. George Watson*: page 12
Henry Benbridge, American, 1743-1812, *The Archibald Bulloch Family*, ca. 1775, oil on canvas, 89 x 66 3/4 in. (226.1 x 169.5 cm), High Museum of Art, Atlanta, Georgia: page 17
Art Resource, NY: William Hogarth, *The Graham Children*: page 19
Ralph Earl, *Elijah Boardman*, The Metropolitan Museum of Art, Bequest of Susan W. Tyler, 1979. (1979.395) Photograph © 1980 The Metropolitan Museum of Art: page 30

Illustrations
All illustrations by Barbara Bedell except the following:
Tiffany Wybouw: pages 11 (middle right; bottom right), 19, 21 (middle left), 26 (bottom left)
Margaret Amy Reiach: pages 8, 25 (middle right)
Bonna Rouse: back cover (arch)
Antoinette "Cookie" Bortolon: page 31

Crabtree Publishing Company
www.crabtreebooks.com   1-800-387-7650

PMB 16A
350 Fifth Ave.,
Suite 3308
New York, NY
10118

612 Welland Ave.
St. Catharines,
Ontario,
Canada
L2M 5V6

73 Lime Walk
Headington
Oxford
OX3 7AD
United Kingdom

Cataloging-in-Publication Data
Kalman, Bobbie
  The milliner / by Bobbie Kalman and Niki Walker; illustrated by Barbara Bedell
       p. cm. -- (Colonial People)
  Describes the work of the milliner in colonial America, which included gown making, laundering, and lace making, as well as selling sewing supplies and other goods.
       ISBN 0-7787-0745-8 (RLB) -- ISBN 0-7787-0791-1 (pbk).
  1. Millinery--United States--History--Juvenile literature. 2. Millinery workers--United States--History--Juvenile literature. 3. United States--Social life and customs--To 1775--Juvenile literature. [1. Millinery. 2. Millinery workers. 3. Clothing and dress--History. 4. United States--Social life and customs--To 1775.] I. Barbara Bedell, ill. II. Title.
TT655.K27 2002
646.5'04'0974--dc21

2001047922

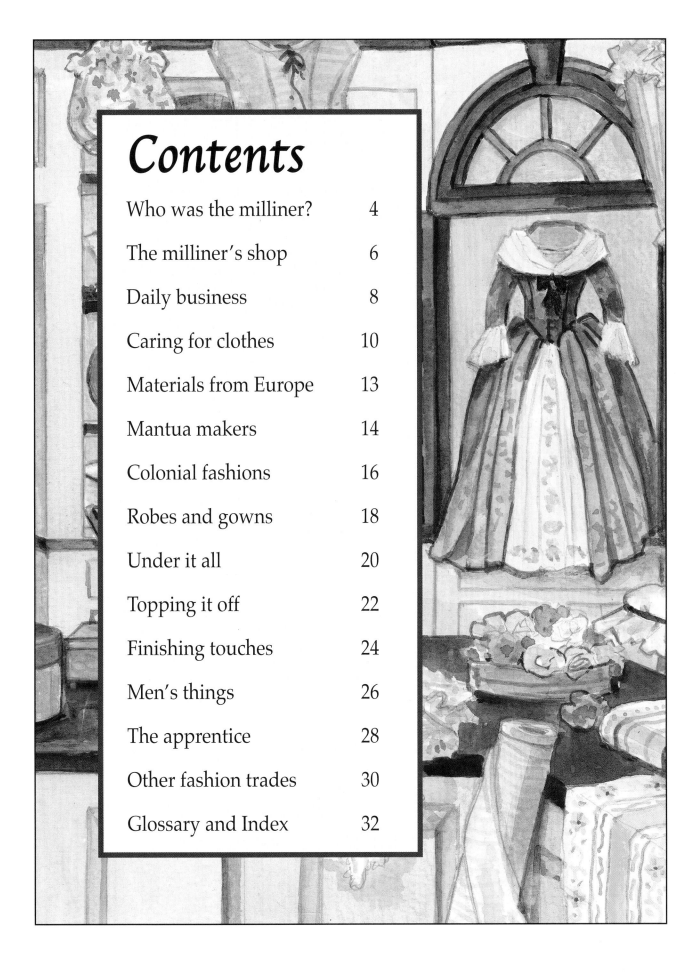

Contents

Who was the milliner?

A milliner was a **merchant** who sold **imported** goods, or goods brought from other places. In the 1700s, North America was made of up **colonies**, or areas that belonged to faraway countries such as England and France. Milliners bought goods made in those places and sold them to the **colonists**, or the people who lived in the colonies. They sold fabrics, thread, trims, hats, purses, children's clothes and toys, cosmetics, jewelry, books, and dishes.

Most milliners were women. A milliner's shop was one of the few businesses a woman could buy and run without a husband. Most other businesses were owned by men and run with the help of their wives.

*Milliners sold men's neckwear such as **stocks**.*

4

Keeping the colonists informed

The colonists were eager to know about the new fashion trends in Europe. It was difficult for them to get this information, however, because there was no regular mail service. They relied on the milliner to inform them about fashion changes.

Milliners bought **merchandise** through **agents** in England, France, and Italy. These agents sent fashion updates, along with the goods they sold to the milliners. Many milliners also ordered magazines showing the latest styles. They provided their customers with a link to "home."

Many colonists dressed well. Women had their own hair styled, but wealthy men never went out without their wigs! The fashion of wearing wigs was started by the French King Louis XIII.

The milliner's shop

Milliners established shops in busy towns and cities. The shops could have a thousand different items for sale! In fact, the word milliner comes from the Latin word *mille*, meaning "thousand." Another source of the word is "Milaner." Fine fabrics and hats sold by the milliner came from Milan, Italy, a fashion center.

The milliner's shop carried merchandise at all prices, so there was something for every woman, whether she was a doctor's wife or a servant. It stocked goods for men as well, such as stockings, handkerchiefs, and tobacco. The more choices a milliner offered her customers, the more goods she was likely to sell.

One-stop shopping

Many customers were in town just for the day and found it more convenient to make one stop at the milliner's shop than to buy items at several shops. Even though **colonial** towns had shoemakers and silversmiths, the milliner also sold shoes and jewelry. Her items were not the same as those sold by local **artisans**, however, since most of her merchandise came from England, France, and Italy.

Look but don't touch!

Milliners stored their merchandise in drawers and boxes to keep it clean. They displayed only a few items and pulled out others when customers asked to see them. In the shop below, many goods are on display to show the variety of merchandise sold by a milliner.

Although the upper classes usually did not shop at the milliner's, they sometimes bought accessories such as fans or bows.

 # Daily business

Oﾠne day was rarely like the next in a milliner's shop. Not only did a milliner sell items the colonists needed, but she provided useful services as well. Some milliners were also **mantua makers**, or seamstresses who made women's **gowns**. They earned more than the milliners who were merchants only.

Offering many services

Most milliners were skilled with a needle. They sewed new garments, mended clothing for their customers, and decorated tablecloths, stockings, and handkerchiefs with **embroidery**, or patterns of fancy stitches. Milliners also cleaned and cared for gowns, which often needed special handling because of the delicate materials from which they were made. They changed the bows and dried flowers on old hats to make the hats look new again.

On the books

At the end of the day, a milliner had to keep track of her business. She kept several books: one recorded anything that was wasted; another listed the **inventory**, or all the goods in the store; one listed the sales made each day. The milliner recorded her **accounts** in yet another book. The accounts showed how much was owed to the milliner as well as the debts she owed. She kept two sets of books—one set at the store and another set elsewhere, in case of fire.

Helping customers

Milliners often placed advertisements in local newspapers to inform colonists that new goods had arrived. Some greeted their customers by asking what they wished to purchase. They then showed the customers samples of the goods that they wanted to buy.

Middling sorts and gentry

A milliner's customers were usually the **middling sorts**, or members of the upper middle class. Members of the **gentry**, or upper classes, bought their fashions directly from merchants in Europe. Many of the milliner's customers were men who were in town for the day on business. Their wives stayed at home on the farm or plantation and gave the men a list of goods to buy. Sometimes men left lists for the milliner to fill while they finished running other errands. At other times, they waited as the milliner showed them a selection of goods.

This milliner is preparing an order for a customer who will return for it later.

9

Caring for clothes

Caring for clothing and hats was an important service provided by the milliner. When she sold a customer a hat, she expected the customer to bring it back to her when it needed new trim. The milliner also cleaned gowns. Some milliners were too busy sewing and serving customers to do this work themselves, so they hired **laundresses**. Laundresses washed and ironed clothes.

Most women washed their **shifts**, shown right, once a week, but they cleaned their gowns only about once a year. Many gowns were made of delicate fabrics that could not be washed. They stayed fairly clean, though, because the cotton shifts women wore under the gowns absorbed sweat.

Laundresses boiled, scrubbed, and rinsed garments by hand. They hung the clothes on a clothesline to dry and then pressed each garment with an iron. They did not wash fine gowns this way.

Tricks of the trade

The boiling water and strong soap used to wash plain cottons and linens would have damaged silks and printed cottons. These fine fabrics needed special care. Today, people take delicate garments to a dry cleaner, but in colonial times, they had to use natural and homemade cleaners.

iron block

Out darn spot!

Milliners and laundresses knew all the tricks for removing stains from delicate clothing. They often cleaned fine fabrics by rubbing them with bread or bran and **powder blue**. They cleaned grease, oil, ink spots, and paint with turpentine, chalk, or lemon juice. If they had to rub out dirt, they did so with a clean wet cloth, followed by a clean dry one. They rolled the damp part of the gown around the dry cloth to keep air and sunlight away. Both faded fabrics.

Women pressed gowns and other clothes with metal irons heated by iron blocks. Several blocks were heated in the fireplace at the same time. When the one in the iron cooled, it was replaced by another from the fire.

Milliners sometimes used a piece of bread to rub out stains in clothing.

Hat care

Just as gowns required special care to look their best, so did hats. Feathers, flowers, and trims became tattered, and curled ribbons went straight. The milliner replaced some of these hat decorations and used a special iron called a **goffer** to put the curl back into the ribbons. A goffer could also be used to recurl hairpieces that had gone straight. The milliner heated the goffer and wound a length of ribbon around it. The heat helped set the curl. She had to be careful not to get the iron too hot, however, or she would singe the ribbon!

Materials from Europe

Ready-made clothing was not considered fashionable, so milliners did not sell finished garments. Nor did they sell locally made fabrics. Instead, milliners carried fine cloth from around the world and sold everything needed to make garments—such as fabrics, thread, buttons, lace, ribbons, and trims.

Imported fabrics

Milliners carried fabrics such as silks from China and cottons from Egypt, India, and Turkey. English merchants bought these cloths and then shipped them to the milliners in North America. Some silks and cottons cost more than others, depending on their color, weight, and quality. Patterned cotton cloth was as expensive as silk because the patterns were printed and painted by hand.

Dyeing the fabrics

Fabrics were colored using natural dyes that came from plants and insects. Some colors were more expensive than others. Green fabric was very expensive because it had to be dyed twice. First the cloth was dyed yellow and then it was dipped into blue dye to make it green. Red dye was the most expensive. It was made from ground cochineal beetles. It took a lot of beetles to make just a bit of dye!

*This milliner is examining a piece of red velvet cloth from which she will make a **cloak**, above. Both this cloth and the dress on page 12 were dyed using beetles.*

Mantua makers

Many milliners were mantua makers, but not all mantua makers were milliners. Larger cities and towns had several mantua makers who worked only at sewing gowns. To attract business, some advertised that they could sew a gown in just one day! Since materials were far more expensive than **labor**, or workers, mantua makers often hired up to five people to help them make a gown.

Custom-made clothes

Mantua makers did not work from patterns. They draped, pinned, and fitted each piece of the garment on a customer before cutting and sewing it. It took up to three **fittings** to get a gown just right. If a woman could not come to the mantua maker for a fitting, the mantua maker sometimes went to her home. At other times, the customer sent her **stays**, which the mantua maker used for measuring the **bodice**, or top part of the gown. Stays were undergarments worn by women. (See page 21.)

(top) After fitting the bodice of the gown, the mantua maker drapes the sleeve. The back pieces and ruffles will be added next.

(below) The customer is thrilled with her new gown. She models it for the proud mantua maker.

In cool weather, women wore cloaks over their gowns. Milliners sold the cloth for cloaks, and some sewed the cloaks as well.

Colonial fashions

Appearances were important to many colonists. People were often judged by their clothing and possessions. Wearing beautiful, fashionable clothes showed people that a colonist was successful and could afford expensive things. Many colonists were eager to wear fine fashions. Families who lived in towns and cities spent a great deal of money on clothing.

*(left) For the first half of the 1700s, the **robe à la française**, or **sacque** gown, was popular. It had long panels that hung loosely from the shoulders. (right) Toward the end of the century, the **robe à l'anglaise** was fashionable. It had a fitted back.*

Wealthy colonists wore fine fashions. Being stylish included more than just clothing, however. A fashionable hostess also owned imported tableware. The milliner sold these goods as well.

Basic styles

Although fashions changed frequently during the 1700s, some basic styles did not change. For instance, men did not wear long pants. They wore short pants called **breeches** that reached just below their knees. They covered the lower part of their legs with stockings. Women wore long gowns with sleeves that covered their elbows. Fashion changes involved new colors, the use of different fabrics and trims, and cutting and draping fabrics in new ways. Milliners made it their business to know the latest styles.

Robes and gowns

A lady's **robe**, or gown, was made up of a bodice, skirt, and one or more **petticoats**. Today, we would call this garment a dress, but in colonial times, "dress" meant "what people wore." It also described formal clothing worn to events such as teas, dinners, balls, and the theater. Everyday clothing was called "undress." The milliner's shop carried everything women needed to make fashionable robes. It also sold fabrics for making "undress" gowns, such as the one on the left.

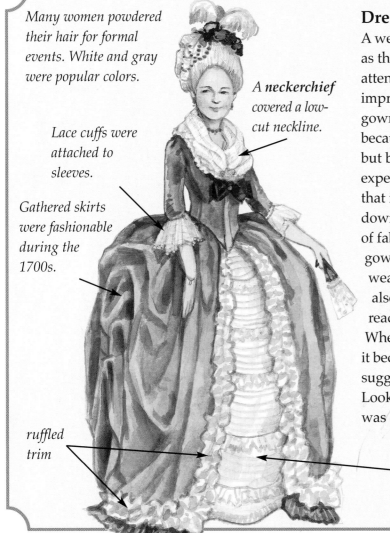

Many women powdered their hair for formal events. White and gray were popular colors.

Lace cuffs were attached to sleeves.

Gathered skirts were fashionable during the 1700s.

*A **neckerchief** covered a low-cut neckline.*

ruffled trim

Dressed to impress

A wealthy woman wore a gown such as this to dress events. Important people attended these events, and she hoped to impress them with her good taste. Her gown was impressive, indeed, not only because it was made in the latest style, but because it required several yards of expensive fabric. The skirt was so wide that it covered two chairs when she sat down! It alone took five yards (4.5 m) of fabric. When people saw this woman's gown, they knew that her husband was wealthy. Her fashionable **accessories** also showed off her wealth. You can read more about them on pages 24-25. When the woman tired of the gown or it became unfashionable, the milliner suggested ways she could update it. Look at page 19 to see how this gown was changed to look new.

*An **open gown** revealed a matching petticoat. A **closed gown** covered the petticoat.*

Girls and babies wore stays and gowns similar to those of their mothers. These young girls are also wearing **stomachers**. Stomachers were triangular decorations that girls and women pinned to the fronts of their bodices. The boy is dressed in the style of his father. When he was a baby, however, he wore gowns, as well.

Staying fashionable

Fashions changed frequently throughout the 1700s, and the changes were good for the milliner's business. Very few women—including wealthy women—could afford to replace their gowns every time trends changed, but they could alter them to suit the new styles. Milliners offered advice on how to update gowns. Old trims could be replaced by fashionable new trims, and gowns could be dyed or embroidered with stylish patterns. Sometimes a gown was taken apart, recut, and put together in a new style. Milliners often made alterations such as the changes that were made to this gown. See the old gown on page 18.

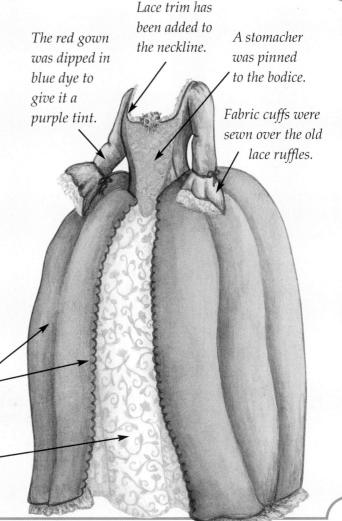

Lace trim has been added to the neckline.

The red gown was dipped in blue dye to give it a purple tint.

A stomacher was pinned to the bodice.

Fabric cuffs were sewn over the old lace ruffles.

*The gathers were taken out of the skirt to make it hang smoothly. Its ruffled trim was removed, and the skirt was cut with a **pinking tool** to give it a fancy edge.*

A new embroidered petticoat replaced the old one.

Under it all

Being fashionable involved more than just wearing the latest the clothing. Women had to be dressed properly underneath their gowns, too! Colonial women wore several undergarments, including a shift, stays, stockings, petticoats, pockets, and **hoops**. Undergarments were made of cotton, linen, or silk. The undergarments of wealthy women were made of finer materials than those of working women, and they owned more of them. The milliner carried a good selection of imported stockings, stays, and hoops at different prices. She also sold the fabric from which underwear was made. Sometimes she embroidered the under-garments to make them look more expensive.

Stays were not supposed to pinch the waist. They were meant to create a smooth, slim shape, improve posture, and support the back. Children also wore stays to help them develop a good posture. The children on page 19 are wearing stays under their clothing.

A woman wore a loose cotton or linen shift next to her skin. It soaked up sweat and kept her gown clean. Many women slept in the same shift they wore all day, but wealthy women had several shifts and changed them often.

There was no elastic to hold up stockings. A woman tied a **garter** above the knee on each leg to keep her stockings from falling down.

A woman wore one or more petticoats over her shift, depending on the weather. Plain **underpetticoats** such as this one were not meant to be seen.

Stays laced up in the front, back, or both. They had strips of whalebone, wood, or metal sewn into them to make them stiff. Some women had their stays made for them by **tailors**. Mantua makers did not sew stays.

pocket hoops

Wide skirts were popular in the 1700s. Women wore metal, whalebone, or cane frames called **pocket hoops** or **panniers** under their skirts to make their hips look wide.

Clothes did not have built-in pockets as they do today. Instead, a woman tied a set of pockets around her waist, over her shift. To put something into her pocket, she reached through slits in the side of her skirt.

Both men and women wore stockings. These long socks reached above the knee and were made of cotton, wool, linen, or silk. Some had fancy patterns, called **clocks**, stitched near the ankle.

21

Topping it off

Hats were worn by both colonial men and women. A woman rarely left the house with a bare head. She wore a cap or hat to keep dust and smoke out of her hair. A man always carried a hat, even if he did not wear it.

People did not wear hats to dress events. Men wore wigs, and women had their hair styled and decorated with pearls, ribbons, and flowers. They often powdered their hair as well. Women tried to save their hairstyles for weeks!

Stylish trims

The milliner sold fancy imported hats covered with stylish trims, but she also carried plain hats. She decorated these hats with ribbons, flowers, and fabrics. By styling the hats herself, the milliner was able to cater to a customer's taste and budget. She could also change the trims on older hats to make them look stylish again.

The huge hat worn by this young woman protects her large, lavish hairstyle, which is hidden underneath. The color of the bow on her hat matches that of the lace on her gloves and sleeves. Her hat matches her neckerchief.

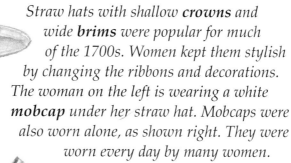

Straw hats with shallow **crowns** and wide **brims** were popular for much of the 1700s. Women kept them stylish by changing the ribbons and decorations. The woman on the left is wearing a white **mobcap** under her straw hat. Mobcaps were also worn alone, as shown right. They were worn every day by many women.

(left) The milliner decorated this hat with ribbons, lace, and silk flowers. Covering straw hats completely with fabric was also fashionable.

Towering hairstyles were popular in the early 1700s. This woman wears a **calash** to protect her hair when she is outdoors. A calash was a stiff hood made of green silk that was gathered over reed or whalebone hoops. The calash was raised or lowered like a carriage top, using strings attached at the front.

Many parents bought their children **pudding caps** to protect their heads. They believed that children could get "pudding head," or soft spots, if they were not wearing these padded hats when they fell down.

The most popular men's hat was the **tricorne**, or three-cornered, hat. Most tricornes were made of fur **felt**.

Many men shaved their heads or cut their hair short so it would fit under their wigs. When not in public, they often covered their heads with small printed or embroidered caps.

Finishing touches

No fashionable outfit was complete without a few accessories. Several types of accessories were popular in colonial times, and the milliner carried a wide variety. She offered her customers advice on which looked best and on how and when to wear them.

More was better

There was no such thing as "too much" when it came to fashion, as the picture on the left shows. This woman is wearing a hat, ruffles, feathers, bows, and a necklace. The neckline of her low-cut dress is covered with a neckerchief and a flower **nosegay**, and her hands are tucked into a stuffed silk **muff** to keep them warm. The small black dot on her cheek is called a **beauty patch**. It hides a smallpox scar. Her lips and cheeks are tinted red with **rouge**. She made the rouge by mixing fat with ground cochineal beetles, which she bought from the milliner.

*Suntans were not fashionable, so a woman always wore **mitts**, left, when she went outdoors. Mitts kept the sun off her hands and arms. In winter, leather gloves kept a woman's hands warm.*

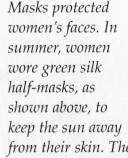

Masks protected women's faces. In summer, women wore green silk half-masks, as shown above, to keep the sun away from their skin. They wore full masks of black silk or velvet in winter to shield their faces from the cold and wind.

Working women wore plain aprons to protect their everyday clothes from stains, but wealthier women wore aprons adorned with lace or embroidery. Women wore these aprons to make a gown look fancier or to give it a new look.

Fashionable women carried silk or paper fans, not only to keep cool, but also to accent their gowns. Young women flirted by fluttering their fans at young men.

Pearl necklaces and **chokers** made with velvet, satin, or lace ribbons were popular colonial jewelry. Some, such as the necklace on the left, carried small portraits. Most necklaces and bracelets were strung on ribbons and tied with bows.

Some ladies carried small handbags to formal events. The purses were made of expensive fabrics and were decorated with beads or embroidery.

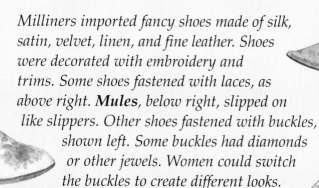

Milliners imported fancy shoes made of silk, satin, velvet, linen, and fine leather. Shoes were decorated with embroidery and trims. Some shoes fastened with laces, as above right. **Mules**, below right, slipped on like slippers. Other shoes fastened with buckles, shown left. Some buckles had diamonds or other jewels. Women could switch the buckles to create different looks.

Men's things

Milliners imported the goods that men needed to be well dressed. Mantua makers did not make men's suits, however. **Tailors** made them. Milliners sold fine fabrics from which the latest styles of jackets, **waistcoats**, and breeches would be made. They also offered a selection of accessories that every fashionable man wore, including hats, stockings, gloves, shoe buckles, handkerchiefs, watches, and **ruffs**, or ruffles, for shirt collars and cuffs. The milliner above is showing a new set of ruffs to her customer.

Stylish men wore embroidered leather gloves, right, when they were riding horses and when the weather was cold. Many carried walking sticks.

walking stick

Men did not wear wristwatches. Instead, they carried their watches in their pockets. The watches were attached to their waistcoats by a ribbon or chain. Watches were expensive, so owning one showed that a man was successful.

Men carried papers in small **pocketbooks** that fit into their jacket pockets. Some were made of colorful fabric, and others were made of leather.

Men's shoes fastened with buckles, just as women's shoes did. The buckles were not permanently attached, so men could wear them on different shoes.

Large, printed handkerchiefs had several uses. Men tied them around their necks, used them to wipe their foreheads, and blew into them after they sneezed.

(left and above) Handkerchiefs were made of linen or cotton. Some were plain, and others had patterns or pictures printed on them.

Finely ground tobacco, called **snuff**, was popular in colonial times. Men sniffed or chewed it. They carried their snuff in small boxes such as the one above. Most men kept a handkerchief handy when sniffing snuff, since it usually made them sneeze.

The apprentice

It took years of learning to become a milliner. Young girls began serving as **apprentices** to milliners around the ages of eleven or twelve. An apprentice learned a trade by living and working with an experienced **tradesperson**. Girls were apprenticed to milliners for five to seven years. Most chose to learn mantua making as well so they could earn more money later. If a girl's family did not own a milliner's shop, her parents chose the milliner to whom she would be apprenticed.

The milliner's contract

An apprentice and a milliner made a contract before the apprenticeship began. The milliner agreed to teach her apprentice the secrets and skills of her trade, such as how to do embroidery and other fine needlework. The milliner also gave her apprentice lessons in basic arithmetic and showed her how to keep track of the expenses and payments in her accounting books. She promised to provide the apprentice with room and board during the apprenticeship.

A fair exchange

By watching the milliner, an apprentice learned how to deal with customers, give advice, and make sales. She also developed a sense of fashion. In return for her education, the apprentice performed many jobs for the milliner, such as running errands, sweeping floors, dusting the shop, and stoking the fire. She was expected to keep the secrets of the trade, behave in a "ladylike" manner, and not leave the shop without permission.

A journeywoman at last!

Finally, after years of learning, the apprentice finished her contract and became a **journeywoman**. A journeywoman was free to work at another milliner's shop or start her own mantua-making business. Many journeywomen stayed on with the milliners to whom they were apprenticed. They began earning modest wages in addition to room and board and could finally begin saving money. Most journeywomen dreamed of opening their own shops.

The apprentice spent hours practicing stitches to perfect her sewing and embroidery skills.

The milliner does needlework as she listens to her apprentice practice her reading. She taught the apprentice the basic arithmetic and reading skills that the girl would need to run her own shop someday.

Other fashion trades

Milliners were not the only tradespeople involved with clothing and fashion. Most towns and cities also had tailors, wigmakers, and shoemakers.

The tailor

Like mantua makers, tailors sewed clothing. Most tailors did not sew gowns, however. They made men's jackets, coats, waistcoats, and breeches, as well as women's **riding habits**, stays, and cloaks. Some cities has as many as fifty tailors!

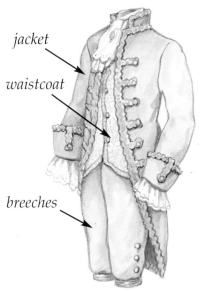

jacket

waistcoat

breeches

This tailor keeps his fabrics in the back room of his office. He advertises his skills as a tailor by the fine suits he wears.

The wigmaker

Wigmakers made wigs and hairpieces for men of the middling sort. They also cleaned and styled wigs, shaved men's faces, trimmed beards, and dressed real hair. To make wigs, wigmakers used goat, yak, horse, and human hair. The wigs came in various styles and lengths and in colors such as white, black, brown, blond, and **grizzle**, or gray. Some had rows of tight curls, and others had a braid or ponytail at the back. Instead of wearing wigs, some men clipped a **queue**, or braid, to the back of their own hair. Women sometimes clipped ringlets, called **curls**, or other hairpieces into their own hair, but very few wore wigs.

The shoemaker

The shoemaker made sturdy shoes and boots for everyday wear. His shoes were usually plainer than those imported from Europe, but they lasted longer. Many dress shoes had cardboard soles, but the shoemaker made his shoes with tough leather soles. He shaped and stitched the shoes around carved wooden **lasts**, which were shaped like feet. He used the same last to make both shoes in a pair, so there were no "left" or "right" shoes. Most shoes from Europe were shaped the same way.

Glossary

account A record of money owed or owing

agent A person who represents another, especially in buying or selling goods

arithmetic The addition, subtraction, division, or multiplication of numbers

artisan A person skilled in a craft

brim The rim or edge of a hat

choker A women's necklace worn tight around the neck

cloak A loose outer garment similar to a cape

cochineal beetle A small red insect, ground to make red dye

colonial Relating to living in a colony or to a period when European countries ruled North America

colonist A person who lives in a colony

colony An area ruled by a faraway country

crown The top of a hat

embroidery Patterns of stitches used to decorate fabric

felt A fabric made of pressed animal hair

fitting The trying on of a piece of clothing to see if it fits properly

imported Describing goods brought into an area or country from another area or country

merchandise Goods bought and sold in a business

merchant A person who buys and sells goods to earn a living

petticoat A skirt worn under a gown

pinking tool A sharp-edged tool used to cut decorative edges along fabric

powder blue A powder that removed stains and prevented white fabric from yellowing

ready-made Describing an item that was already sewn and ready for purchase

riding habit A matching jacket and skirt worn for horseback riding

shift A loose-fitting dress worn against the skin and under clothing

silversmith A person who made silver items

stays A woman's undergarment that gives the waist and upper body a smooth shape

tailor A person who sews men's clothing and some women's garments

tradesperson A person who has an occupation that requires special training or skill

underpetticoat A skirt worn under a petticoat

waistcoat A men's vest, which was worn underneath a jacket

Index

1 2 3 4 5 6 7 8 9 0 Printed in the U.S.A. 1 0 9 8 7 6 5 4 3 2